Amazing Animals
Deer

Please visit our web site at www.garethstevens.com
For a free catalog describing our list of high-quality books, call 1-800-542-2595 (USA) or 1-800-387-3178 (Canada).
Our fax: 1-877-542-2596

Library of Congress Cataloging-in-Publication Data

Wilson, Christina.
    Deer / by Christina Wilson.—[Rev. ed.]
          p. cm.—(Amazing animals)
      Originally published: Pleasantville, NY : Reader's Digest Young Families, copyright 2006.
      Includes bibliographical references and index.
      ISBN-10: 0-8368-9115-5   ISBN-13: 978-0-8368-9115-7 (lib. bdg.)
      ISBN-10: 1-4339-2119-7   ISBN-13: 978-1-4339-2119-3 (soft cover)
    1. Deer—Juvenile literature. I. Title.
    QL737.U55W555 2009
    599.65—dc22   2009000238

This edition first published in 2010 by
Gareth Stevens Publishing
A Weekly Reader® Company
1 Reader's Digest Road
Pleasantville, NY 10570-7000 USA

Executive Managing Editor: Lisa M. Herrington
Senior Editor: Brian Fitzgerald
Senior Designer: Keith Plechaty

Produced by Editorial Directions, Inc.
Art Direction and Page Production: The Design Lab/Kathleen Petelinsek and Gregory Lindholm

Consultant: Robert E. Budliger (Retired), NY State Department of Environmental Conservation

Photo Credits ©
Front cover: Digital Vision; title page: Nova Development Corporation; contents page: JupiterImages; pages 6–7: Digital Vision; pages 8, 11: Corel Corporation; page 12: Digital Vision; pages 14–15: PhotoDisc, Inc.; page 16: © iStockphoto.com/James Phelps; page 18: Jhaviv/Dreamstime.com; page 19: iStockphoto.com/David MacFarlane; page 20: iStockphoto.com/Vladimir Ivanov; page 21: JupiterImages; pages 22–23: PhotoDisc; page 24 (inset): Nova Development Corporation; page 24: JupiterImages; page 27: iStockphoto.com/Jeffrey Noble; page 28 (upper left): iStockphoto.com/Lawrence Sawyer; page 28 (lower left): JupiterImages; pages 28–29: Dynamic Graphics, Inc.; pages 30–31: iStockphoto.com/Michael and Michelle West; pages 32–35: © Brand X Pictures; pages 36–37: Corbis Corporation; pages 38–39: JupiterImages; page 40: Corbis Corporation; page 43: Dynamic Graphics, Inc.; pages 44–45: JupiterImages; page 46: iStockphoto.com/Lawrence Sawyer; back cover: Nova Development Corporation.

Printed in the United States of America

1 2 3 4 5 6 7 8 9 14 13 12 11 10 09

Amazing Animals
Deer

By Christina Wilsdon

Gareth Stevens
Publishing

Contents

Chapter 1
A Deer Grows Up.. 7

Chapter 2
The Body of a Deer... 15

Chapter 3
A Deer's Antlers 23

Chapter 4
A Deer's Year 31

Chapter 5
Deer in the World 39

Glossary 44

Show What You Know.................................... 46

For More Information................................... 47

Index 48

Chapter 1
A Deer Grows Up

A **fawn** weighs from 5 to 9 pounds (2.3 to 4 kilograms) when it is born.

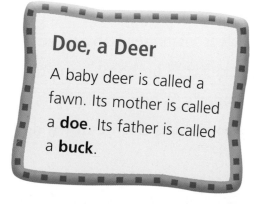

The baby deer blinks as she looks at the world around her. She is only a few minutes old, so everything is brand-new to her. She sneezes as a blade of grass tickles her nose. Suddenly, something warm and wet washes over her face! It is her mother's tongue, busily scrubbing her from head to toe.

The mother deer came to this quiet spot to give birth. This is the mother's first fawn, but she already knows how to take care of her baby. She licks the baby deer dry, then lies down next to her. The baby nuzzles close and drinks her first meal of milk.

Soon the baby struggles to her feet. She wobbles on her long legs. By the time she is an hour old, the baby can walk. When she is about five hours old, she follows her mother away from the place where she was born.

Doe, a Deer

A baby deer is called a fawn. Its mother is called a **doe**. Its father is called a **buck**.

The mother deer leads her baby to a grassy spot in the woods that has many leafy plants. There the baby lies down, curls up in a ball, and flattens her ears against her neck. She blends in so well that she seems to disappear!

Before quietly stepping away, the mother deer nuzzles the baby. She looks back once to make sure her baby is safely hidden. Then the mother deer heads off to find food.

The baby deer naps. When she awakes, she looks around but stays still. She knows that lying quietly is her best protection. A hungry animal passing by is less likely to notice the baby if she doesn't move.

Many animals use their sense of smell to find their next meal. A fawn gives off no smells for a **predator** to sniff. To keep her own smell from her fawn's hiding place, the mother deer stays away as much as possible. But she is always close enough to hear the baby if she **bleats** or cries. If a predator comes near, the mother will lure it away from her fawn.

The mother deer visits her baby three or four times a day to feed her. The baby leaps to her feet and nurses eagerly. When the baby is done feeding, the mother makes her lie down again.

Hard to Spot
A fawn's coat is dotted with about 300 white spots! In the woods, the spots make it more difficult for a predator to see the fawn, especially when the sun shines among leaves.

Coats of the Seasons

White-tailed deer have summer and winter coats. Their coats change color so the deer will blend in better with the colors of their **habitat**. In summer the deer are red-brown, and in winter their coats turn either tan or bluish gray.

One day, when the fawn is almost one month old, her mother does not make her lie still. Instead, when the mother starts to walk away, she bleats softly. The fawn jumps to her feet and follows her mother into the woods. Now the fawn travels everywhere with her mother. She tastes the leaves that her mother eats.

The baby also meets other deer for the first time. She sees a pair of fawns running after a doe. This doe is her grandmother! The baby plays with the other fawns while the does feed.

The fawns run and jump. They shove one another and play tag. They chase butterflies and stamp their hooves at rabbits.

Summer turns into fall. The baby's coat is changing. Her white spots have worn away, and the color of her fur is turning from red-brown to tan or gray. She eats only plants and no longer nurses.

The mother and baby stay together all winter. In the spring, the mother deer chases her baby away before giving birth to her second fawn. In the summer, they pair up again. The fawn and her mother will stay together for many years, separating only to have their babies.

Chapter 2
The Body of a Deer

High Jump

Deer can leap about 30 feet (9 meters) in just one bound and can jump over a fence 8 feet (2.4 m) high!

Leaping Legs!

If you were standing still in the woods, a white-tailed deer could sneak right past you with barely a sound! Its thin, long legs carefully and quietly tiptoe over roots and rocks. Its slim body slips between tree trunks. If you make the slightest noise, the deer will race away in leaps and bounds.

A deer can run up to 35 miles (56 kilometers) per hour for short distances—that's about as fast as a racehorse. When a deer runs on soft soil or through light snow, it leaves heart-shaped hoofprints behind. The sharp hooves of white-tailed deer are used to kick and slash predators.

Big Deer, Little Deer

White-tailed male deer are larger and heavier than the females. A buck in the northern part of North America usually weighs from 150 to 200 pounds (68 to 91 kg)—about the weight of an average man. A very big buck may weigh up to 300 pounds (136 kg)!

The smallest white-tailed deer are the Key deer. They live in a part of Florida called Big Pine Key. A Key deer weighs about 70 pounds (32 kg)—the size of a German shepherd.

Sensing Danger

Deer use all their senses to detect danger. Animals such as wolves and cougars hunt them for food. Humans also hunt them.

Deer constantly listen for the slightest noises. The size and shape of their ears help them hear faint sounds, just as cupping your hand behind your ear helps you hear better. A white-tailed deer can point one ear forward and the other one backward at the same time. The snap of a twig is enough to send a deer bounding for cover.

A deer is quick to see motion. Its eyes sit high up on the sides of its head. This allows it to see forward, backward, and to either side!

A deer sniffs the air while feeding to make sure no predators are close by. It uses its nose to smell which plants to eat.

Hightailing It!

A white-tailed deer's tail is as long as a 12-inch (30-centimenter) ruler and is fluffy white underneath. When a deer is frightened, it flips up its tail. The flash of white warns other deer of danger. A doe's white raised tail helps her fawn follow her when there is little or no light.

A white-tailed deer can turn its ears in all directions to listen for the slightest sounds of danger!

White-tailed deer eat up to 10 pounds (4.5 kg) of food per day!

Time to Eat

White-tailed deer wander in woods and fields, eating the leaves of many plants. They also eat small stems, nuts, bark, grass, and fruit. Deer like the vegetables and fruits that grow on farms. They will even visit people's gardens to eat flowers.

A white-tailed deer has no upper front teeth, but it can still nip off leaves and twigs. It simply grabs them between its lower front teeth and a tough pad on its upper jaw. Then it chews the food off. It often leaves behind stems with ragged, chewed tips.

A deer uses its back teeth to crush food briefly before swallowing. Then the food enters the first part of the deer's four-part stomach. Later, the deer coughs up the food as **cud**. It chews this cud thoroughly and swallows again. Feeding this way lets a deer eat quickly while it is out in the open, where danger lurks. Afterward, when the deer feels safe, it can relax while it chews.

The chewed cud travels through the deer's **digestive system**. It can take up to one and a half days for a meal to be digested.

Favorite Food

Of all the foods that deer eat, they like apples best.

Chapter 3
A Deer's Antlers

Antlers or Horns?

Antlers and horns are not the same thing. Every winter antlers fall off, and new ones grow back in the spring. Horns remain on animals year after year.

This young buck has two points on each antler. This makes him a four-point buck. He is also known as a Y buck, because each antler looks like the letter Y.

A Rack of Antlers

Every spring, bumps appear on the heads of white-tailed bucks. These bumps are the beginnings of antlers. They sprout from two knobs, called **pedicles** (PEH-duh-culz).

The antlers are made of solid bone, but at first they are not shiny and smooth. They are covered in a fuzzy, warm skin called **velvet**. It is warm because it is filled with blood vessels. The blood nourishes the antlers as they grow. By late August, the antlers are fully grown. The velvet begins to dry up and fall off. The bucks help peel it off by rubbing their antlers on trees or by scraping the antlers with their hooves. Antlers can measure 3 feet (1 m) from tip to tip.

Wild Words

A **rack** is a pair of antlers.

Total Points

A buck is more than a year old when he grows his first antlers. They are usually just single spikes, and the buck is called a spike buck. When the buck starts to grow antlers with more points, he is called a rack buck. Older bucks have larger antlers and more points than young bucks. One buck grew antlers with 78 points!

Rack Attack

When a buck looks for mates in the fall, he is friendly to the does he meets. He is not as friendly to other bucks. When two bucks meet, the weaker one often leaves. If he does not, then the two bucks will probably fight.

First, the bucks look directly at each other and walk toward each other on stiff legs. The furry hairs stand up on their necks and backs. The bucks flatten back their ears and turn their heads to show off their antlers. They stab at bushes and paw the ground with their hooves. Then, heads lowered, they charge.

Antlers crash. The two bucks push and shove with their heads. Each one twists his neck as he tries to flip his opponent onto his side. Eventually, one buck gives up and runs away.

Antler Drop

In midwinter, the antlers of a buck fall off. First one drops, then the other. A buck with one antler will usually lose the other in a day or two. The raw, red spots on his head will heal quickly.

The shed antlers are nutritious and do not go to waste. They are eaten by chipmunks, mice, and other small creatures.

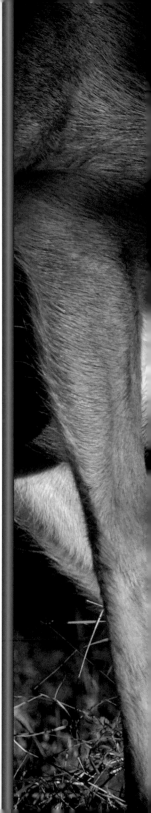

White-tailed bucks use their antlers to fight other white-tailed bucks for mates or territory.

The mule deer looks a lot like a whitetail, but it has huge ears and a black-tipped tail. The branches of the mule deer's antlers divide into smaller branches with points. A whitetail's antlers each have one main branch with points.

Each antler of a male elk can be 5 feet (1.5 m) long! Elk are also called wapiti (WAH-puh-tee). They live mainly in the Rocky Mountain states and southern Canada.

The moose is the world's largest deer. It is about as big as a horse and weighs more than 1,000 pounds (454 kg)! The male's antlers are wide, flat, and huge.

Different Deer Antlers

Deer antlers vary in size, shape, and design. Different kinds of deer grow different kinds of antlers, although many antlers have an overall similar shape. There are about 45 different **species** of deer in the world! The Eld's deer of Asia has huge antlers. The antlers often have between 12 and 20 points.

Five species of deer, including the whitetail, are native to North America. Their first **ancestors** were born in the region thousands of years ago and were not brought by settlers from other lands.

Unlike other members of the deer family, both male and female caribou (also known as reindeer) grow antlers. The male's antlers are bigger than the female's.

Caribou antlers have a shape that's a bit like the shape of a human hand, with a palm and fingers. Caribou live mainly in Alaska and Canada.

Chapter 4
A Deer's Year

A doe having her first fawn usually gives birth to just one baby. Older does usually have two fawns at a time. Some does have three or four!

Spring and Summer

Spring brings new leaves and grass for deer to eat. The food grows just in time for the does, who are ready to give birth.

All winter, different families of does live together as one big herd. Each family is made up of a doe, her daughters, and all their fawns. In the spring, the oldest doe chases her family away. She needs to be alone for her fawn's birth. Her daughters will also give birth alone.

In summer, does and fawns form family groups again. The does eat while the fawns play. On hot days, they lie in the shade, panting like dogs. They are most active at dawn, dusk, and night.

The does watch out for danger. If a doe is alarmed, she snorts loudly and stamps a front hoof. This is a warning to other does. They instantly look, listen, and sniff the air.

The bucks do not join the does. They form small bands made up of bucks only. They also spend spring and summer eating. Some of the food nourishes new antlers as they grow. The bucks often butt heads with one another, pushing each other with their antlers. For now, these shoving matches are partly for fun. They also help the bucks test to see who is strongest before the mating season begins.

Autumn

Autumn is mating season for white-tailed deer. It is also the does' last chance to fatten up for the winter.

By now, fawns have stopped nursing and are eating plants. They follow their mothers, nibbling on leaves, berries, twigs, and stems. The deer also feed heavily on autumn crops of acorns and beechnuts.

The bucks do not spend much time eating. They are ready to find mates. The bands of bucks who have been friends all summer have split up. They no longer **spar** with one another. But a buck may still spar with a bush, hooking his antlers into the branches and stabbing at it from all sides.

A buck also rubs his antlers against trees as he searches for does. He is not rubbing the velvet off. That task has been completed. He is rubbing his antlers on trees to mark them with his scent and to scratch off bark. This turns the tree into a signpost, warning other bucks that he is in the area. This signpost is called a **buck rub**. He also scratches the ground with his hooves, making marks called scrapes. The does sniff the rubs and scrapes to find out about the bucks, too.

A doe will run away
from a buck until she
is ready to mate.

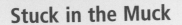

Stuck in the Muck

The size and shape of deer legs make it difficult for deer to walk in deep snow or mud. The deer sink and become stuck. If a deer falls on ice, it has trouble standing back up. It has difficulty on the slippery surface, just as you might!

This buck won't have his antlers much longer. In winter, bucks lose their antlers as well as their interest in does and fighting.

Winter

By winter, white-tailed deer have shed their red-brown coats. Now they wear thick winter coats of tan or bluish gray. People often say winter deer are "in the blue."

This thick coat slows down the loss of heat from the deer's body. It **insulates** the deer from the cold just as a winter coat insulates a person. It holds in heat so well that if snow falls on a deer's back, the flakes do not melt!

Heavy snow blankets the land in the most northern places where white-tailed deer live. Winter in these places is hard for deer. They have difficulty traveling in the deep snow. Food is scarce.

Does and fawns survive the winter by forming big herds in sheltered places. This is called yarding up. The deer stay together in the yard for protection from wind and snow. They leave the yard to find food. As they come and go, they stamp out paths through the snow that lead to patches of food.

In very cold winters, deer may find only bark and evergreen needles to eat. If necessary, deer will stand on their hind legs to reach twigs, bark, and needles high up on trees.

Chapter 5
Deer in the World

The Best Habitat

White-tailed deer can survive in different habitats—forests, fields, and swamps. The best habitat for whitetails is a place with both fields and woods. There they can feed in the fields and run to the woods for safety.

Where White-Tailed Deer Live

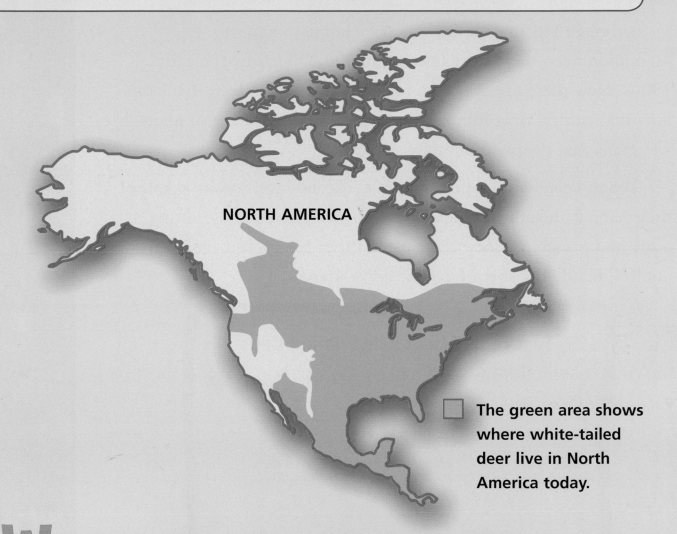

NORTH AMERICA

The green area shows where white-tailed deer live in North America today.

White-tailed deer are one of the most common big land mammals in North America. They live almost everywhere in the United States (except Hawaii, Alaska, and parts of the Southwest) and across southern Canada. Whitetails also live in Central America and parts of South America.

The Future of Deer

Although North America was once home to almost 40 million deer, there were fewer than 500,000 left by the early 1900s. Now there are about 20 million white-tailed deer, thanks to laws that control deer hunting. In some places, there are so many whitetails that people think they are pests.

Today, keeping deer populations at a good level means keeping their habitats healthy. In some areas, this can be done by setting aside and protecting their habitats. In other places, it means controlling the number of deer that live there.

Fast Facts About White-Tailed Deer

Scientific name	*Odocoileus virginianus*
Class	Mammals
Order	Artiodactyla
Size (not including tail)	Males: up to 7 feet (213 cm) Females: up to 5½ feet (168 cm)
Weight	Males: to 300 pounds (136 kg) Females: to 200 pounds (91 kg)
Life span	2 to 10 years in the wild 20 years in captivity
Habitat	Forests, fields, swamps
Top speed	35 miles per hour (56 kph)

You Can Help!

Become a member of a **conservation** group that works to protect deer habitats. It may even be your local zoo.

Glossary

ancestor—a member of a family that lived many years before

antler—a bony structure that grows from the head of male deer

bleat—to make a sound like a cry or whimper

buck—a male deer

buck rub—a tree marked by a male deer with scent and scratch marks from its antlers

conservation—the protection and preservation of land, animals, plants, and other natural resources

cud—a ball of partly chewed plant food coughed up by a deer for more chewing

digestive system—part of the body that processes food

doe—a female deer

fawn—a baby deer

habitat—the natural environment where an animal or plant lives

insulate—to cover something so that heat is kept in

pedicles—knobs on a male deer's head from which antlers grow

predator—an animal that hunts and eats other animals to survive

rack—a pair of antlers

spar—to practice fighting without harming the opponent

species—a group of living things that are the same in many ways

velvet—fuzzy skin that covers a male deer's growing antlers

Deer: Show What You Know

How much have you learned about deer? Grab a piece of paper and a pencil and write your answers down.

1. **What is another name for a baby deer?**

2. **How long does it take for a baby deer to learn to walk?**

3. **What color coat do deer have in summer?**

4. **How fast can deer run?**

5. **What is the name of the smallest kind of white-tailed deer?**

6. **What is a deer's favorite kind of food?**

7. **How many different species of deer are there in the world?**

8. **What happens to antlers after the deer shed them?**

9. **Why do antlers feel warm when they are covered in velvet?**

10. **What kinds of habitats do deer live in?**

1. Fawn 2. About an hour 3. Red-brown 4. Up to 35 miles per hour (56 kph) 5. Key deer 6. Apples 7. About 45 different species 8. They are eaten by chipmunks, mice, and other small creatures 9. The velvet is filled with blood vessels 10. Forests, fields, and swamps

For More Information

Books

Gray, Susan Heinrichs. *Key Deer* (Road to Recovery). Ann Arbor, MI: Cherry Lake Publishing, 2007.

Kalman, Bobbie. *Baby Deer* (It's Fun to Learn About Baby Animals). New York: Crabtree Publishing, 2008.

Stefoff, Rebecca. *Deer* (Animalways). Tarrytown, NY: Benchmark Books, 2007.

Web Sites

NatureWorks: White-Tailed Deer

www.nhptv.org/NATUREWORKS/whitetaileddeer.htm

Find out more about the white-tailed deer and its characteristics, life cycle, and habitat.

World Deer

www.worlddeer.org/index.html

Learn about all kinds of deer living throughout the world, including the Père David's deer, a species that almost died out.

Index

A

antlers 24, 25, 26, 27, 28, 29,
    33, 34
autumn 26, 34

B

baby deer 8, 9, 10, 12, 13, 32
birth 9, 13, 32, 33
bucks 9, 17, 24, 25, 26, 27, 33,
    34, 36

C

caribou 29
coats 10, 12, 13, 37
color 10, 12, 13, 37
communication 10, 13, 33, 34

D

danger 18, 19, 33
digestive system 21
does 9, 13, 18, 32, 33, 34, 35,
    37

E

ears 18, 19, 28
eating 10, 13, 20, 21, 34, 37
Eld's deer 29
elk 28
eyes 18

F

fawns 8, 9, 10, 13, 32, 33,
    34, 37
female deer 9, 17, 29, 42
fighting 26, 27, 33, 34, 36
food 10, 13, 20, 21, 34, 37

G

group behavior 13, 33, 37

H

habitats 17, 28, 29, 40, 41,
    42, 43
hooves 17, 25, 26, 33, 34
hunting 18, 42

K

Key deer 17

L

legs 17, 36
life span 42

M

male deer 9, 17, 42
mating 26, 27, 34, 35
moose 28
mother deer 9, 10, 13
movement 13, 16, 17, 18, 36
mule deer 28

O

odor 10

P

pedicles 25
playing 13
points 24, 25, 28
populations 42
predators 10, 17, 18

R

rack 25, 26
reindeer 29

S

size 17, 28, 42
smell 10, 18, 19
sounds 10, 13
speed 17, 42
spring 13, 24, 25, 33
stomach 21
summer 12, 13, 25, 33

T

tails 18, 28
teeth 21

V

velvet 25

W

wapiti 28
weight 8, 17, 28, 42
winter 12, 13, 26, 33, 36, 37